A Weapon Called the Word

To Jeanne

Thanks for your support,
I hope you enjoy!.

Love,
Steve
CX

Steven Michael Pape

Published by

ROSE BOOKS
Affiliate of Avenue U Publications
2015

QUEENS   BROOKLYN   LONDON
ROME   SAN FRANCISCO

"Steven further demonstrates his poetic intelligence with 'A Weapon Called The Word'. His poetry remains engaging whilst seamlessly switching between local matter, and that of more distant worlds, always with the subject matter at heart in the most evocative way – splendid!"

- Aron Kirk-Poet-
Explosions in Thailand,
Alabaster diary

"Steven Michael Pape reflects the gritty realism of English punk: the poverty the angst, the unrest. Its abhorrence of saccharine pop culture is laid bare in his verse, unapologetically challenging the reader to look under the surface of contemporary society."

- Dave Wolff-
AEA Zine,
New York

"Steven joined the Wolf International Poetry Exhibition in 2017. His poetry prompts one to examine social justice and to come to a decision within as to the current state of affairs in the UK, and other parts of the world, regarding poverty, homelessness, corruption and more. His words are worth reading. 5 stars!".

-Villayat
'Snowmoon Wolf'
Sunkmanitu

"Steven has a way of seeing things from the underdogs point of view, and his style of rhyming and thoughts are well worth reading.
His reflections on real life such as 'Generation despair', 'Wasteland', 'Death of a homeless man' are interesting and thought provoking.
As is 'Death by media', a sympathetic look at the life of Amy Winehouse and how she was haunted by the press."

-Robert Attewell
Editor- Ilkeston Life

"Some poets learn their craft in class. At college. From fellow poets. But when you read the work of Steven Michael Pape, you see someone who refined his trade at the school of real life. His poetry is about punk rock, unemployment, drugs, knife crime. When you read his compelling sentences, you get a feeling of someone who's lived the life. Learned his pentameters on Ilkeston's streets not a writing course. In short, he speaks for the working people of the East Midlands. And how many poets can honestly say that? Pape writes with a down-to-earth style, in verse uncluttered by pretension. This lets his honesty shine through. A poet for everyone, I find Pape easy to read, meaningful and memorable. I think you will too."

-Ian C Douglas.-Author
- writer, author and creator of
the Zeke Hailey book series
www.iandouglas-writer.com

"We're the flowers
In the dustbin
We're the poison
In your human machine."

-Sex Pistols.
God Save The Queen.

Contents:

Introduction   8
    by Rose Cirigliano

Words   16
A weapon called the word   17
A tax-funded buffet.   18
Drunk on the knowledge   19
Hazy day   20
Changes   21
The quiet room   22
Street scene   23
Skeleton shoes   24
Life won't wait   25
Faceless I watch   26
A broken down daydream   27
Wasteland   28
The remnants of revellers   29
The alienation of a generation   30
Small Town solidarity   31
Museum of the past   32
World view   33
We wear a mask   34
Society makes me sad   35
Death by media   36
Spring is now upon us   38
Concrete   39
Starvation wages   40
Hope in a hopeless world   41
Generation despair   42
The train keeps rolling   43
Walking up the down escalator   44

Eyes of the City   45
Room Twenty-Four   46
Stand up,unite   47
A strange little Town   49
Look at us all   51
Sunday swings   52
Death for a postcode   53
Skin is skin   54
Death of a homeless man (England 2018)   55
Disillusioned   56
Silent snow   57
Gentleman Ged   58
I am not an Artist   59
Push the Boundaries   60
Third Generation Punk   61
Twenty-seven   63
This is England   64
The view from the morning   65
In the early hours   66
Through worlds apart   67
Babylon Calling   68
Time   70
Walk   71
Consuming.   73
He keeps Artist hours.   74
Seize the Day   76
Plastic Transparency   77
The Future   79

About the Author   **80**

Other Works   **83**

INTRODUCTION

> If you would be a poet, create works capable
> of answering the challenge of
> apocalyptic times, even if this meaning
> sounds apocalyptic.
>
> You are Whitman, you are Poe, you are Mark
> Twain, you are Emily Dickinson and Edna St.
> Vincent Millay, you are Neruda and
> Mayakovsky and Pasolini, you are an
> American or a non-American, you can
> conquer the conquerors with words....
>
> — Lawrence Ferlinghetti.
> From *Poetry as Insurgent Art*
> *[I am signaling you through the flames]*.

If ever there was a need for consciousness raising, it is now. Steven Michael Pape's contribution to this mission is on every page of this book. Each of his poems captures a moment in time where we pause in reflection with him, perceiving layers of reality founded on an underlying wisdom that makes us aware of ourselves as a society of conflicted individuals that need to pass on hope for the future to the next generation, our children.

Steven is to "punk" what Ferlinghetti is to "the beats"; their poetic voice expressing the conscience.

True to the movement, Steven works outside the mainstream, enjoys a following in his town, as well as working with other artists and having his work in several exhibitions, and is a "do-it-yourselfer" self-publishing his works.

It has been my pleasure to work with him on this particular publication, which I found to be a collection of insightful observations. Steven's words are so perfect. I could see, hear, and often times even smell the scene he created. The rhythm of the works is easy and almost calls for some music at times.

Declaring his intent from the first poem, "A weapon called the word." The collection continues with a series of poems; "A tax-funded buffet.", "Drunk on the knowledge", "Hazy day", and "Changes" that describe the world over the course of time, painting a picture of the reality of life in the streets of his home. Portraits of the inhabitants as in "The Quiet Room" further clarify the poverty and sadness that provoke his words. These observation spill out into the street in "Street Scene" and "Skeleton Shoes" leading to the urgency expressed in "Life won't wait" and the despair expressed in "A broken down daydream",

We are shattered, in fragments,

Like porcelain dolls, with empty eyes,
The whiteness a contrast,
To the blackness of the ground.

The society Steven speaks of is beautifully drawn in "A broken down daydream," "Wasteland" and "The remnants of revellers."

In "Alienation of a Generation" we see the reasons behind this war with words; poverty and injustice.

It's time to smash the system,
Whilst it's still on its knees,
As the mass media amplifies,
With its childlike greed.

But as the young now rise up,
They're all hearing their voice,
As they now show the world,
That they do have a choice.

A broader and more universal perspective is offered in the next group. "Small Town solidarity," "Museum of the past," "World view."

As we now lie wide awake,
Is this a nightmare or dream?.
Our minds seem confused,
No inner strength to scream.

In "Society makes me sad," and "Death by media," Steven drags us into the 21st Century and the impact of gossip columnists and the paparazzi on the lives of the famous.

> *And we'll make up some lies,*
> *To see your name in print,*
> *To then sell to the red tops,*
> *We're all making a mint.*
>
> *Your life is our life,*
> *We're completely obsessed,*
> *We hear you're exhausted.*
> *You've no time for rest.*

Expressing our frustration intermingled with hope is found in the next group; "Spring is now upon us," "Concrete," and "Starvation wages."

> *We try our hardest it takes all our might,*
> *To find the strength to stand up and fight,*
> *But the system has us it's taken us over,*
> *We're never any richer only much older.*

And the hope?

> *Is there hope in a hopeless world?,*
> *Banging our heads against crumbling walls.*
> *That inner voice, that wants to scream out,*

But there's no sound there at all.

And as we view the poverty, the despair,
Under a thin veiled view of society.
That the mass media force feed us,
All lies, in different varieties.

The ebb and flow of life in the streets, poverty, homelessness, drunkenness, older generation and new....all beautifully drawn in the ensuing group. "Concrete," "Starvation wages," "Hope in a hopeless world," "Generation despair," "The train keeps rolling," "Walking up the down escalator," "Eyes of the City," "Room Twenty-Four," "Stand up, unite," "A strange little Town," "Look at us all," "Sunday swings," "Death for a postcode."

From the "Silent Snow" on we see a mission form until the final anthem and challenge to stand up and fight the good fight.

If we push the boundaries,
They will finally move,
If our voices are heard,
It shows we've something to prove.

We don't need any violence,
We just don't play that way,
We're much better than that,

At the end of the day.

And at protests and demos,
Pacifist's from the heart,
We don't need to raise our fists,
We look for the finish at the start.

And some final tributes to the prophets that have gone before…

And this voodoo child, a guitar that sings,
A sixties hero with gem-stone rings,
The purple haze running so deep,
As you finally find restful sleep.

A hippie showing her strong female force,
All shown in her gravel edged voice,
This pearl of wisdom, just so progressive,
Yet your deadly habits became too aggressive.

This lizard king, with his poet shamen roar,
Writhing drunkenly over every stage floor,
And the Paris days as you tried to find your way,

*A solitary bath, growing cold was your
last day.*

*The Grunge soul with a life of
complications,
Showing your angst for the lost
generation,
Such lyrical beauty, these words of
despair,
Those shotgun shells, a final note you
prepare.*

*A bee-hive lady with her wounded dark
eyes,
Trying to find escape from night until
sunrise,
Those rehab dreams, never again to
wake up,
Lying lost, alone, with mascara
smudged make up.*

To fully appreciate this collection, I suggest you read it in several sittings. You will need time for pondering.

- *Rose Terranova Cirigliano (editor)*

THE WORDS

A weapon called the word.

A weapon called the word
Our hidden thoughts, underneath.
The escapism of the mind
On the paper, it secretes.

We shout out at the system,
But we don't need no violence
As we write our inner ideas
Our weapon, is never silenced.

We are the lost people,
That the Government collate
Into their neat little boxes
Through frustration, we relate.

We are the lost artists,
But you don't know our names.
Graffiti spray in the suburbs,
Our message is never the same.

We're the new generation
Putting our anger into print
But our souls are still alive
As we write, what we think.

We are the voices from the streets
Our message is one of freedom
Our weapon is our words
More than before, we need them.

A tax-funded buffet.

So they're clearing up the streets,
For the big Royal occasion,
Moving the peasants out the way,
In a huge clean up operation.

Can you go and stand round the corner,
You scruffy looking twat,
The posh people are arriving,
In Armani suits and strange hats.

A tax-funded buffet,
But we can't have any cake,
These money grabbing manipulators,
That we all helped to make.

A televised debacle,
Of comedic proportions,
That's came out of our pockets,
A mass screening abortion.

And look at that dress,
It's so expensive, elegant,
I can see why my taxes,
Rose by pounds and not pence.

But it's good for the nation,
I've heard some people say,
Doesn't London look beautiful,
With the homeless out the way?.

But Meghan's Dad won't be attending,
He's told a bit of jackanory,
And Harry's won't be either,
But that's another story......

Drunk on the knowledge.

We all got drunk on the knowledge,
As we sat on the bar-stools of life.
We all tasted the bitter sweet,
And felt the embers, called strife.

And we recalled all conversations,
Of those now so long passed.
Our memories were still visual,
And those faces, always last.

And as we drank the sweet wine,
We all laughed and joked until dawn.
Amongst the beauty of the flowers,
All of us, were the thorns.

We burnt the candle at both ends,
Burning the middle as well.
As we tasted the joys of heaven,
And felt the wrath of our own hell.

And we shook hands as we parted,
Into the dark infinity of the night.
But our minds were still alive,
With the experience of our life.

We were all drunk on the knowledge,
Our brains bruised, with our words.
As we vacated into the darkness,
Our minds were faded, disturbed.

Hazy day.

Another hazy day,
Just waking up,
Burnt, black toast,
Chipped coffee cups.

In other rooms,
The sunlight lays,
Across the silent forms,
Of sleeping babes.

And in the garden,
The pale blue sky,
The sun is shining,
As the Aeroplanes fly.

A breath of fresh air,
As nature now calls,
A folded out chair,
Against a crumbling brick wall.

As cats wander round,
To find a strip of sun,
Their hazy days,
Are never really done.

And in the early nighttime,
With the door ajar,
The bats are flying around,
But there not getting very far.

As the sky now drops dark,
And the moon starts to wane,
These long hazy days,
We'll hopefully see again.

Changes

I spent so long just watching,
A lone spider spinning its web,
For the cruel winds to destroy it,
And place it in my path to tread.

With the sun highlighting the weeds,
The sunflower sheds its petals,
Providing a rare burst of colour,
Amongst the stark stinging nettles.

As the birds camp out on t.v aerials,
Singing into the pale sky,
The neighbourhood cats are peering,
With their strange, watchful eyes.

The trees are picking up the breeze,
Swaying gently with subtle sound,
It adds to the changing ambience,
That I can now feel all around.

And shouts echo from the streets,
Drowned out by motorcycle roars,
As aching and tired feet,
Are all walking broken tarmac floors.

And as the sun is now being replaced,
By the clouds as black as ink,
Toning down all my thoughts,
And diluting everything I think.

The quiet room

In this quiet room,
With get well cards,
The creams and pills,
In tubes and jars.

And hand-drawn pictures,
Created by small hands,
Bright colourful pictures,
Depict the sea and sand.

There's a pale form,
Cocooned in the sheets,
Calm and so peaceful,
Entering the big sleep.

The window is open,
Such a subtle breeze,
The soul has now flown,
On its final release.

Street scene.

The bus shelters smashed,
All the metal's twisted,
Scarred with words,
The paintwork, blistered.

These streets are paved,
In broken glass,
In dog excrement,
And used zip-lock bags.

The rain is so cold,
As it soaks to the bone,
Cars splash the people,
As they're heading home.

The mopeds roar,
In no safety clothes,
Their bare heads ready,
To hit the dirt filled road.

All the dirty puddles,
Soak through our cheap shoes,
As run down shops,
Advertise cheap booze.

Every street you travel,
You can smell the weed,
As children run riot,
All these mouths to feed.

And the food smells,
Seem to invade the nose,
Yet our empty pockets,
Fulfill our foes.

And as the night goes black,
The street-lights now stream,
A low cost lighting,
Onto our street scene.

Skeleton shoes.

With skeletons on my shoes,
Through these streets I roam.
Listening out for the vocal cries,
That echo from broken homes.

All the shattered glass,
Embedded deep into my soul,
As I pray for the sun,
To shine on my aching bones.

And the anguished voices,
From these drunken mouths,
No inner realisation,
What the argument's about.

Now hanging in the parks,
The youths are smoking Spice,
All catatonic stares,
From their dead fish eyes.

Outside the pubs,
The smokers talk and stand,
The heavy duty drinkers,
The nine-thirty a.m gang.

And as the nightfall arrives,
Bringing its darkest hues,
These streets seem uneven,
Walking in skeleton shoes.

Life won't wait.

Life won't wait,
For traffic lights,
For nightmare dreams,
In the dead of night.

Life won't wait,
For ticking clocks,
For hot water bottles,
And old bed socks.

Life won't wait,
For the young or old,
For the tune it plays,
We all sing the song.

Life won't wait,
For the fear inside,
For those shaky hands,
Holding sharpened knives.

Life won't wait,
For our indiscretions,
For our lack of empathy,
Our own misdirections.

Life won't wait,
For us to hold its hand,
For the time trickling down,
Depicted by the sand.

Faceless I watch.

Standing on the top of the old Church tower,
Daylight creeping up in this slow skylight hour,
The people below are like miniature ants,
I feel like a voyeur watching their dance.

This precipice between life and death,
Between the unknown and the angels breath.
This ancient crumbling stone,
Has now become my own secret tomb.

Everyone unaware of my high existence,
As I hover on this old stone ledge,
Far below me are the headstones,
All the faded spirits lying long dead.

This sublime peace from up in the air,
As all this sunlight glistens stark and bare,
And the Church bells now start to chime,
Telling all the faceless the right time.

It's market day coloured canopies below,
Red, green and then yellow all in a row,
The slight breeze carries fruit sellers cries,
Only just audible to my ears in the sky.

As I climb down and join the masses below,
The crowd in swarms, ending in a huge flow,
I gaze back up longingly at the Church tower,
And reminisce of my time alone for that hour.

And as I look up and study the ancient roof,
I remember that time when i tasted the truth,
When up in the sky, and alone for a while,
Secret was my existence, and faceless my smile.

A broken down daydream.

Our bodies were broken,
Splintered like old furniture,
That pierces the bare feet,
Of unsuspecting people,
Blood loss and anguished screams.

We are shattered, in fragments,
Like porcelain dolls, with empty eyes,
The whiteness a contrast,
To the blackness of the ground.

There's vomit on the street,
A Pollock pavement recital,
And faded blood from a fist fight,
A stark vision of a useless generation.

People in 4x4's oblivious,
Heading for lost destinations,
Broken brains, swarming like bees,
Destroying the atmosphere,
With over-priced petrol pollution.

The eyes are a window to the soul,
Smashed like the faded factories,
Of our yesterdays, now occupied,
By the bones of skeleton squatters.

The people are all blindfolded,
Their shoulders a huge weight,
Head down to the reality, the horrors,
A poison pill keeps the demon at bay.

A broken down daydream,
Observed with watering eyes.

Wasteland

Houses are being built,
On every bit of wasteland,
Low cost and high rise,
Cheap bricks and sand.

The vandals spray the walls,
With poorly spelt words,
The To Let signs are broken,
Lying splintered, disturbed.

And the pubs are kinda grimy,
There's a feeling of lost hope,
The kinda places that,
Have cracked sinks and no soap.

The smell of stale beer.
And a thousand late nights,
Of lock ins and laughter,
And sometimes a fist fight.

And through this wasteland,
Of pale and tired faces,
With their dreams of a better life,
Different Town, different places.

And the scratchcards and booze,
Paid for by the dole,
Bringing home the bacon,
Along with the toilet rolls.

The smashed glass shines,
On this place of despair,
Walking through this wasteland,
Ignoring all the stares.

The remnants of revellers.

The streets are empty, devoid of humans,
Even the obligatory dog walkers,
Are safely ensconced, behind drawn curtains.

As people piece together last nights antics,
A reassembling of the brain, hot coffee and tablets.

And the early morning streets, are littered,
With the remnants of revellers, crushed cans,
Vomit, a wine bottle perched on a gate post.

Blood from a fall, or fight,
Pizza boxes and fried chicken bones,
Wet and discarded in the rain.

And as I walk through the rain swept streets,
It seeps through a hole in my boot, soaking my sock,
As I curse aloud into the empty streets,
My voice echoing off the houses of sleeping occupants.

The alienation of a generation.

The alienation of a generation,
Our wages low, house prices high,
They're now wrecking the economy,
Right before our eyes.

Mass capitalism and profit,
All now well beyond dispute,
As we sit in run down houses,
With our ever leaking roofs.

A share in prosperity?,
Our citizens don't have a clue,
These funds are so limited,
For me and for you.

Now all divided politically,
Between the young and the old,
A nation that no longer believes,
Those lies they've been told.

The penny pinching manipulators,
Now seen for what they are,
A big house in the country,
And their chauffeur driven car.

It's time to smash the system,
Whilst it's still on its knees,
As the mass media amplifies,
With its childlike greed.

But as the young now rise up,
They're all hearing their voice,
As they now show the world,
That they do have a choice.

Small town solidarity

Small Town solidarity.
'Good morning, Sir,
ain't it bloody nippy?
there's a bit of snow in the air'.

From pubs escapes the laughter,
A cacophony of voices,
The football on the wide screen,
The bookies offering their choices.

And the market traders stand,
In six layers of clothes.
Selling their odds 'n' ends,
A hanky held to every nose.

The solidarity is in the people,
And the choices they have to make,
From the rent they have to find,
To low paid jobs they have to take.

And even when they're skint,
There's still a smile from their lips,
A friend offering their help,
And enough drinks to sink a ship.

The faces may be hardened,
But that's the life that they have led,
Growing up in poverty,
Five kids sharing one bed.

You see this is the kind of place,
Were people make amends,
Where that person at the bus stop,
Once a stranger, is now a friend.

The museum of the past.

And as we all walk down these halls,
Living in the museum of the past,
Our reality may seem jaded,
But our memories, are surpassed.

As we then recall our childhood,
And all those lost innocent ways.
Those everlasting summers,
And the never ending days.

And all our minds were so free,
Not troubled by the adult world.
We seemed to survive in a vacuum,
Like since the day we became uncurled.

Still we all walk down these halls,
Observing the textures, the colours,
Our memories are still alive,
Because of our Fathers, our Mothers.

This museum it never closes,
And these thoughts they never quit.
This is the museum of our past,
And we all still walk through it.

World view.

As we now lie wide awake,
Is this a nightmare or dream?.
Our minds seem confused,
No inner strength to scream.

And as we view the world,
In our own subtle surprise,
Our brains can't function,
Behind our Codeine eyes.

All our thoughts are eclipsed,
We now struggle to think,
As we await the destruction,
Our world view slowly sinks.

We can't make any sounds,
From our own muted mouths,
We can't summon up the energy,
To stand, let alone shout.

But we continue to move forward,
Because the past can't be relived,
And as the future stretches before us,
All we can do now is forgive.

We wear a mask.

We wear a mask & a uniform,
In our daily employment,
We smile at our orders,
We feign fake enjoyment.

We become what our bosses,
Conceive us to be,
Following the instructions,
Behind our eyes, apathy.

This is not the real persona,
It's a watered down dream,
With our list of demands,
Mouths trying not to scream

And we keep a lid on emotions,
To keep a roof over our heads,
We need food on the table,
The kids safe in their beds.

But this uniform doesn't fit,
And the mask it slowly slips,
This desk and computer,
A chair in which we sit

And our patience grows thin,
Our eyes adjusting to the light,
Praying for some salvation,
From Morning until Night.

Society makes me sad.

Society makes me sad,
Armed police on our streets,
Reading all the headlines,
In stunned disbelief.

Society makes me sad,
The kids hanging in the parks,
Taking deadly drugs,
When night-time turns to dark.

Society makes me sad,
Politicians made of plastic,
Turning a once calm scene,
Into one that's now drastic.

Society makes me sad,
The homeless on the street,
Each hand that's held out,
Making them worthless, underneath.

Society makes me mad,
The broken concrete of the streets,
Hate, anger and war,
When all we want is peace.

Death by media

Death by media,
The flash-bulbs roar.
Look into our cameras,
Not at the floor.

We now own your life,
That we helped to make,
We're so cunning and wise
Like a poisonous snake.

We'll talk to your friends,
To fill out our pages.
We'll go through your bins,
You cannot escape us.

And we'll make up some lies,
To see your name in print,
To then sell to the red tops,
We're all making a mint.

Your life is our life,
We're completely obsessed,
We hear you're exhausted.
You've no time for rest.

We are the vultures,
And we like what we see.
Your life through our lens,
Our total apathy.

And we'll capture your worst,
But discard your best,
Just look at those eyes,
Wide open, distressed.

And now look at this photo,
The pallor of the skin,
This fame once a blessing,
Soon becoming a sin.

And even in death,
We'll highlight your mistakes.
As you sleep the big sleep,
The deadly media, awakes.

**Remembering Amy Winehouse

Spring is now upon us.

Spring is now upon us,
Those first clear mornings.
As the snowdrops are now rising,
The bird's orchestra is calling.

Life in the canvas of nature,
Helps to induce our reflection.
The start of Spring, invigorating,
Helps our quiet contemplation.

The yellow of the Daffodils,
Growing wild in the woods,
Adding contrast to the trees,
A touch of colour to the mud.

Washing is hanging on the line,
Pegged out by an early riser,
And as the people walk their dogs,
Their moods are seeming much brighter.

There's a crispness in the air,
That tells us Spring is now approaching,
To rid us of all those dark nights,
That consumed us, all encroaching.

And with the greening of the grass,
The last trees are now unfurled,
Warmed by the sun, then rain,
Spring is arriving, uncurled.

Concrete.

I see a man lying down
He's seemingly fast asleep
Using his arm as a pillow
And for his bed, this concrete.

And he sometimes gets help
Of a hot drink or a roll
It inflates his dead heart
Puts some hope in his soul.

But there's some that are unkind
To this lonely lost man
Those that are so cruel
And will kick his face if they can.

He stays awake in the night
When this City grows dark
Spending those long hours
Hiding out in the park.

He prefers to sleep in the day
When the people are around
He's got used to the traffic
And the strange City sounds.

But the Councils won't help him
Spending their money on sculptures
To bring in the tourist trade
And make this bleak City seem cultured.

And he bears so many scars
From each year on these streets
For now though he sleeps
On his bed of concrete.

Starvation wages

Starvation wages keep us keen,
Tired and hungry, slaves to a machine,
Early morning with the wind and rain
Different day but destinations the same.

The clock machine sucks our soul,
It opens up to devour us whole.
Time is our enemy we wish it away,
Hoping and praying for the end of the day.

We try our hardest it takes all our might,
To find the strength to stand up and fight,
But the system has us it's taken us over,
We're never any richer only much older.

Metallic grind of the same old machine,
Lacklustre light, a variable smokescreen,
Our voices unheard in suffocated silence,
Heads all down as we work to compliance.

Empty pockets are making idle hands,
A cigarette break, a bucket of sand,
Dust and grime and mass pollution,
Starvation wages, is there another solution?

Hope in a hopeless world.

Is there hope in a hopeless world?,
Banging our heads against crumbling walls.
That inner voice, that wants to scream out,
But there's no sound there at all.

And as we view the poverty, the despair,
Under a thin veiled view of society.
That the mass media force feed us,
All lies, in different varieties.

Is there belief in a poisoned world?,
Just virtual reality in a headset.
The mass escapism of a generation,
An alienation of the mindset.

And all these hopeless ideals,
Hidden behind a queue of cynics.
And all those empty pages,
Left discarded by the critics.

Hope in a hopeless world,
All the nightmares and daydreams.
These plastic,fake,monopoly money,
Indestructible,and wipe clean.

Generation Despair

You can sense it on the streets,
You can smell it in the air,
You can see it in the faces,
Generation despair.

No one wants the factory,
No one wants to be there,
No one can escape,
Generation despair.

And those in the dole queue,
And those that don't care,
And those red-tape liberals,
Generation despair.

Can you see the interrogation?
Can you see the chair?
Can you see the questions??
Generation despair.

Poverty for the homeless,
Poverty for souls laid bare,
Poverty for the working,
Generation despair.

Hope in those desperate,
Hope in those with flair,
Hope in those hopeless,
Generation despair.

Those that continue fighting,
Those that even dare,
Those that question everything,
Fucking Generation despair!.

The train keeps on rolling.

This train it keeps on rolling,
There's no red lights, only green,
And as these thoughts all materialise,
Some are beautiful, some obscene.

These tracks stretch on for miles,
There's no beginning and no end,
And as we enter the tunnels,
We're all going around the bend.

And you can't vacate this journey,
Or even hide behind a disguise,
The conductor comes a calling
Wherever you hide, he will find.

And as we pull the emergency stop,
So that we can finally escape,
The train just keeps on moving,
It doesn't slow down, it accelerates.

And there's no end to this journey,
Although so many have tried,
All those weary travellers,
With their lost, insomniac eyes.

This train just keeps on rolling,
Full of all our images and words,
When it finally gets derailed,
It's by those lost, disturbed.

Walking up the down escalator.

We all walk up the escalator,
That always seem to be going down,
All our memories are hazy,
And our heads stuck in the clouds.

As we now view all the creatures,
From our strange vantage point,
All the mouths are opening,
As all the faces, contort.

And we seem as though we're walking,
Through tons of thick sludge,
This heavy weight on our shoulders,
We seem unable to budge.

Yet this machine does not stop,
The loud grind of the coil,
We all try to walk through it,
Yet it only adds to our toil.

The mechanics do not stop,
From this hard steel floor,
Our legs pumping furiously,
But too heavy to take more.

We all still walk up the escalator,
But it's always going down,
As our brains now all recoil,
We seem perplexed,profound.

The Eyes Of The City

The eyes of the City,
Tall buildings loom.
As hands dirty like the earth,
Hold cold coins of pity.

The cracks in the paving stones,
Like the dark recesses of our mind.
A safe place to escape into.
The sirens of the City, pierce the air,

As the laughter escapes the pubs,
A thousand swollen livers,
Embracing the late night license.
The homeless man, holding,

Creased editions of the Big Issue,
Eyes showing hope, yet deep despair,
Is etched into his face,
Showing the pavements abuse.

The eyes of the City,
Are like the eyes of the old,
Watchful yet sometimes vacant,
Observing the human circus,

As dirty puddles reflect our image,
Like the fairground mirrors,
Of our childhood, distorted.

Room twenty-four

In room twenty-four,
The atmospheres strange,
The framed photos on the wall,
At odd angles,not arranged.

There's a single bed,
Pale blue, and un-made,
A chair in the corner,
In a similar shade.

A sink and a mirror,
With faint toothpaste smears,
A faded old photograph,
That depicts younger years.

A clock on the wall,
Still ticking away,
It's a hour behind time,
But that don't matter today.

The view through the window,
A vast field of green,
With the trees swaying softly,
It's all looking serene.

And this floor has been walked on,
By so many different feet,
All moving so slowly,
With a new day to greet.

But room twenty-four,
Won't stay vacant for long,
A new soul will soon grace it,
Waking up to the birdsong.

Stand up, unite.

All my Brothers and Sisters,
There's no need to fight,
Ya know what i'm saying?,
Stand up, unite.

We all breathe the same air,
And face the same plight,
We don't need the violence,
Stand up, unite.

The press try to label us,
As the black or the white,
Through their pages of ignorance,
Stand up, unite.

Through all of these streets,
From the Morning till Night,
We all face the same struggles,
Stand up, unite.

There's been too many deaths,
Caused by corrupted minds,
We don't need to add to them,
Stand up, unite.

From a Father and Mother,
We all came into this life,
As we all try to evaluate,
Stand up, unite.

We don't need any hatred,
To make everything right,
Stand together in solidarity,
Stand up, unite.

Through all these generations,
There's been mass divide,
It's time for a new outlook,
Stand up, unite.

And we don't need no conflict,
As we all fight the same fight,
Can we fight it together?,
Stand up, unite.

Don't listen to the media,
Or the fools of the far right,
We all know the truth,
Stand up, unite.

These shackles that binds us,
From our own freedom fight,
We now need to break them,
And stand together, unite!

A Strange Little Town.

This is a strange little Town,
There's plenty of eccentrics,
The bus drivers getting told off,
By card carrying geriatrics.

And we've a Punk window-cleaner,
Who calls everyone,'Ken',
Once you have seen him,
You won't forget him again.

There's a bloke called Trooper Hunt,
Dressed in full army camouflage,
He's on his own special mission,
But he won't do you no harm.

And if you walk up Bath Street,
Without gasping for breath,
You're a true Ilkestonian,
It's kind of a test.

When you get to the top,
You'll see St. Mary's at full height,
The door standing open,
If you're looking for the light.

And there's plenty of cafe's,
Serving full English with a slice,
'Get that down ya duck,
it'll soon put ya right'.

Saturday at the football,
With loads of rowdy noise,
Six-hundred plus supporters,
Shouting for the Ilkeston boy's.

Yes, there's a rise in unemployment,
It's not just reminiscent of here,
The youths sitting aimlessly,
Drinking super strength beer.

We've now got a train station,
But we used to have three,
It's still handy for the shoppers,
Who want to visit the City.

And Bennerley Viaduct,
That opened in 1878,
The Germans tried to bomb it,
But left it too late,

The structure was too strong,
They couldn't move that out the way,
It's still standing as a testament,
To this very day.

It's an old mining town,
People once slaved in the dark,
There's a mock-up of the head-stocks
Visible over Shipley Park.

And the Industries might be gone,
But the people remain proud,
There's no time for self-pity,
It's not really allowed.

And just like any place,
It's had its ups and its downs,
But i'll always call it home,
This strange little Town.

Look at us all.

Look at us all,
Rushing about,
Off out to work,
Putting the bins out.
Driving like maniacs,
To get to a place,
That if we died tomorrow,
We'd soon be replaced.
Clocking into factories,
With impending doom,
Starting a new week,
That's arrived much too soon.
Working and sweating,
Old bones turned to dust,
To survive in this world,
That we do at a push.
To pay rent or mortgage,
A roof over our heads,
Cash for a big T.V,
New mattress, old bed.
A loan that we'll pay,
Till we're one hundred and five,
That job, occupation,
That eats us alive.
Wishing our life's away,
One day at a time,
At the foot of the hill,
But a long way to climb.
Yet we continue to do it,
Before poverty calls,
Rushing like lunatics,
Just look at us all.

Sunday Swings.

Sunday swings towards the quiet,
The car-washers with buckets,
The dog walkers, the bikers,
Soap suds in the roads,
Washed down the drain,
The smell of people's dinner,
It's always the same.
Some people are still sleeping,
Behind every locked door,
The atmospheres so different,
From the day before,
All anticipating the next day,
When the working week starts,
Leaving the warmth of a bed,
To commute in the dark.
The lunch-time drinkers,
Sit with their hair of the dog,
A few swift pints,
To help rid the head fog.
And the church doors are open,
As the Vicar checks his watch,
Awaiting the congregation,
The arrival of his flock.
Yes, Sunday has a silence,
Unlike any other day,
It swings more towards the quiet,
It's always been this way.

Death for a postcode.

Death for a postcode,
Knives in young people's hands,
The papers print their headlines,
The public struggles to understand.

Killed for a territory,
Maimed for life for drugs,
The young with no conscience,
A prison sentence, a shoulder shrug.

And six stabbings in one day,
Down in London Town,
The figures then show us,
That Police numbers are down.

Hooded youths are running wild,
Bricks aimed at those in authority,
The people wearing black,
Outnumbered by the majority.

Can we blame unemployment?,
Or a lack of things to do?.
Should we blame their upbringing?,
I really don't have a clue.

A wall sprayed with gang graffiti,
Police tape wrapped like a shroud,
Fresh blood on the pavement,
As the sirens are ringing loud.

The young killing the young,
With death for a postcode,
A knife, a fashion accessory,
None of them growing old.

Skin Is Skin.

Skin is skin,
A heart is a heart,
If our skin's white as ivory,
Or as black as the dark.
If your accent is clipped,
I really don't care,
If you've been born here,
Or from way over there.
You see, we bleed the same colour,
We feel hurt and pain,
Hatred is self hatred,
There's nothing to gain.
Ignorance isn't bliss,
It's intelligence turned low,
There is no argument,
There's nowhere to go.
The power is in the people,
Respect should be in us all,
What can we gain,
From a faded slogan on a wall?

Death Of A Homeless Man
(England, 2018)

The temperature is below freezing,
There's old cardboard on the ground,
A homeless man is shivering,
In a thin tent that now surrounds,

Pitched up against a wall,
In a darkened church yard,
A sleeping bag that's ripped,
And a bed that's cold and hard.

Released from a hospital,
Just a few weeks before,
No forwarding address,
Just released and ignored.

There is no humanity,
When Government's close doors,
When any visit to a City,
Means seeing people on the floor.

Begging for some change,
With a scrawled cardboard sign,
A degradation of the soul,
And a sad state of our times.

And the papers print the bare facts,
'The Death Of A Homeless Man',
And then we read the next day,
That it's happened yet again.

Disillusioned.

This nation as a whole has lost contact with reality,
Force fed their existence through social media society,
Through the vortex to the whirlpool of despair,
Hurtling somewhere, disconnected without due care.

And at a certain hour as dusk was close to falling,
All the creatures were hollering and then calling,
Arriving on time but like uninvited guests,
Invading our presence, dirtying our flesh.

A journey into the desert with no return,
Apathy and stagnation were there to learn,
Our downfall occured, a plummet to the floor,
Senseless abandonment has got us once more.

The penetrating gaze that will materialise,
A trauma of intrusion in our lost eyes,
An act of defiance raises from the abyss,
Accumulated words echo from empty lips.

We're disillusioned with a little run down concern,
It's from these decisions that you finally learn,
I've been debased through every association,
Hostility arises from each cheap limitation.

Engaged in the system, experience can only grow,
Insight portrayed through dramatical flow,
A semblance of normality, perceiving the clarity,
The plight of a man in an unjust society.

Silent snow

The sky is pure white,
It matches the ground,
As the snow gets heavier,
All silent, profound.

There's a calm to the colour,
It's better than the rain,
There isn't that noise,
As it hits window panes.

The bird's in the trees,
Sit on skeletal arms,
There echoed chorus,
Adding musical charms.

The children are excited,
As they dig out their boots,
Cartoon hats and scarves,
And all-in-one suits.

The grass pokes through,
Adding colour to the white,
The garden of serenity,
A vibrant, colourful sight.

Stepping out onto the yard,
Where nothing will now grow,
The cold on our faces,
All around us, silent snow.

Gentleman Ged.

You were like a bright spark,
With mischievous eyes.
Always funny and kind,
As bright as the sunrise.

And every little thing,
That people helped you with,
You were always so courteous,
Always willing to give.

So rare in a human,
That ability to always smile.
A soul so infectious,
That stretched on for miles.

So kind and so warm,
A handshake to greet,
A nice conversation,
To every person you did meet.

Your soul was much larger,
To those that could see,
For those that appreciated,
Your true empathy.

And your memory will live on,
In ways that's so loud,
That terrace cheer you still hear,
Down at Ilkeston Town.

So as you rest in the clouds,
As kind words are now read,
You will always be remembered,
As Gentleman Ged.

In memory of Ged Tatham

I am not an Artist.

I am not an artist,
My hands don't drip with paint,
I don't use a canvas,
What I see, I write, collate.
It's pure observation,
It's in everybody's head,
It wakes you in the early hours,
As your brain is still in bed.
It's confusing and there's no answer,
There is no right or wrong,
It's a film you may have seen,
Or in the lyrics of a song.
It's fingernails on a chalkboard,
As thoughts escape from a dark mind,
Thinking about world peace,
But knowing it will forever be unkind.
A Eulogy that you've written,
An oak coffin for the dead,
A vicar in a dog-collar,
As the sentences are read.
I don't feel as though I've earned it,
With the word artist as a title,
Scrawled words on creased paper,
A hoarse voiced, nervous recital.
I don't need a handshake,
Or a friendly pat on the back,
I don't need club membership,
To remind me of the fact,
That I am not an artist,
So don't confuse me for one,
I am just a deep thinker,
When all is said, and done.

Push the boundaries.

If we push the boundaries,
They will finally move,
If our voices are heard,
It shows we've something to prove.

We don't need any violence,
We just don't play that way,
We're much better than that,
At the end of the day.

And at protests and demos,
Pacifist's from the heart,
We don't need to raise our fists,
We look for the finish at the start.

We question what we know is wrong,
Authorities with their jaded ideas,
We listen to all of their lies,
And observe the faces, full of fear.

Their fear of the crowd, fear of the masses,
We're publicly proud, socially too strong,
With our cacophony of voices,
We fight against what we see as wrong.

Third Generation Punk.

Johnny Rotten was singing about the Queen,
The crowd, obnoxious, spitting, obscene,
I was too young to experience it at all,
To see the slogans sprayed on the wall.

Sid Vicious with his spiky hair,
And his rabbit lock, he really didn't care,
A legend for his generation,
A life lived fast through punk frustration.

And when I grew up, older mates would say,
You should of been there in the day,
The beer was cheap & the bands were great,
I'd listen envious as they would relate.

And by the 90's when I could go,
I saw The Ramones twice in a row,
And absorbed the lyrics and the clothes,
Joey and Johnny striking a pose.

I saw Joe Strummer in another band,
He had the crowd in the palm of his hand,
And the crowd all wanted 'Hammersmith',
We stood, transfixed as the first note hit.

And The Sex Pistols reformed in '96,
That was a gig I just couldn't miss,
In Finsbury Park on a Summer's day,
A pint of piss was thrown my way,

And when the opening song was ringing out,
My heart I swear was in my mouth,
Total chaos, everyone acting obscene,
For me it was a punk rock dream.

And even now, as I'm growing much older,
In mosh pits, people over my shoulder,
And I see the young starting out,
Drunk & reckless, jumping about.

A new generation, the music won't die,
'Punks not dead' The Exploited still cry,
You can never kill anything that's so strong,
A third generation Punk, is that so wrong?.

Twenty seven.

This founder with long, suffering eyes,
Rolling stoned for most of his time,
Then motionless, lost in deep water,
A faded genius, a lamb to the slaughter.

And this voodoo child, a guitar that sings,
A sixties hero with gem-stone rings,
The purple haze running so deep,
As you finally find restful sleep.

A hippie showing her strong female force,
All shown in her gravel edged voice,
This pearl of wisdom, just so progressive,
Yet your deadly habits became too aggressive.

This lizard king, with his poet shamen roar,
Writhing drunkenly over every stage floor,
And the Paris days as you tried to find your way,
A solitary bath, growing cold was your last day.

The Grunge soul with a life of complications,
Showing your angst for the lost generation,
Such lyrical beauty, these words of despair,
Those shotgun shells, a final note you prepare.

A bee-hive lady with her wounded dark eyes,
Trying to find escape from night until sunrise,
Those rehab dreams, never again to wake up,
Lying lost, alone, with mascara smudged make up.

This is England

This is England.
The racists crawl out the woodwork again,
This time though it's not screams or shouts,
A Polish man killed by a group of layabouts,
Killed just for speaking in his native tongue,
Beaten to death whilst on the phone.
And the far-right groups with banners of hate,
Preaching a message that's so out of date,
And knives are held by much younger hands,
To kill for a postcode or to join a gang.
And yet the Government war still rages on,
Amidst all this carnage are bodies and bombs,
Terrorism threats for some unknown cause,
Praying to the Koran and to a supposed higher lord.
And poverty seeps from everyone's pores,
Vast unemployment and zero hours clause,
Children run wild in the wind and the rain,
The parents at home out of their brain,
Old people getting mugged for a Heroin fix,
To help stop the sickness, or to cure the itch,
And the Government's crooked just like before,
There's money to be made by going to War,
Young soldiers arrive home in a mental state,
What they had seen they're too scared to narrate.
The homeless with dirty hands all now held out,
They haven't the strength to stand up and shout,
Wanting salvation from some kindly soul,
Before the cold of the street devours them whole,
But people rush past them or speed past in cars,
This is England, we all bare your scars.

The view from the Morning.

The view from the Morning,
Heavy rain and high weeds,
The birds are perched on fences,
Looking down for worms on which to feed.

The trees all standing high,
Moving slowly with a gentle breeze,
The branches that were once empty,
Are now full with virgin leaves.

And the neighbourhood cats,
Shelter under broken benches,
Waiting for the rain to subside,
So they can continue their adventures.

On these rain soaked streets,
People standing and talking,
Under their fragile umbrellas,
As they then continue their walking.

The sewers discard all the water,
Mixed in with debris, dirty leaves,
A strong smell of decay,
Washing over our sodden feet.

And the view from the Morning,
Soon turns into the afternoon,
Bringing with it much darker clouds,
A picture painted of impending gloom.

In the early hours.

In the early hours is when creativeness flows,
The twilight entities and the crescent moon glows,
With our paper cuts we're all writing in blood,
And showing our inner ideas just like we should.

Yes, the Poets are crazy, the artists are too,
With their abstract creations, paint thickening like glue,
With their canvas they portray their inner thoughts,
And the poet with ideas, their words are there art.

As the pen glides across its a slippery slope,
We think of old dreams, past memories and hope,
And we think of the past, the present, and the future,
All of these things help to make up the structure.

And in the early hours it's the best time to write,
A time to exorcise the memory let it take full flight,
And open up pandora's box full of all these ideas,
And distinguish the demon as it reappears.

Through worlds apart.

Through worlds apart feeling condemned in the heart,
All the bitter words confused, left out in the dark,
The journey we take, always leaving so much at stake,
The immortal decisions that we're forced to partake.

The essences in themselves seem to now sing,
Like the dawn birds' chorus signalling Spring,
From the lightest corners to the darkest recess,
The imagination moves at the slightest caress.

Yet as we continue we don't view all the faces,
The shadows behind us firmly left in their places,
The red dimmed glow, lights all of our ways,
From daylight to dusk, the concrete dismays.

A vanished illusion in our sublime dreams,
Strange concocted visions we've always seen,
Straining to see in the darkness, the light,
The lost embraces of the lovers at night.

The broken earth directs us to primal days,
Our pupils dilated in the fire of our haze,
With melancholy fashion, dazzling in passion,
The motionless existence we now fail to fathom.

Babylon calling.

The babylon are now calling,
But they're never knocking light,
Your front doors been moved,
Six feet from last night.

They're now invading your house,
And shouting loud in your face,
As you stand there in your dressing gown,
Wiping the sleep off your face.

And they don't like your skin colour,
And your house they says a mess,
Getting close up in your face,
Putting your patience to the test.

They're looking for some contraband,
Or a nice bundle of cash,
Is there a receipt for this t.v?,
Or do we really have to ask?.

Please sit down on your settee,
Because we're searching very hard,
We've got a trained sniffer dog,
Just waiting in your backyard.

Are you working at the moment?,
And can I smell drugs in here?,
Did you leave this house last night?,
You smell strongly of stale beer.

And please don't shout at me,
It shows the guilt in your eyes,
We're acting on information,
That you've something you want to hide.

Yes, the babylon come knocking,
A large riot van parked in your street,
They may creep up to your door,
But they're never really discreet.

Time.

We seem to waste our time, we don't appreciate,
That time can be cruel, we just can't relate.
Time is slow for prisoners pacing their cells,
Time is pain for those living in hell,
There's little time left for the ill dying in beds,
Or time for the relatives, all those words left unsaid.

Time can be a saviour, yet an enemy too,
Either flowing like water, or sticking like glue,
And at work the time seems to be standing still,
With the excess of laughter, too much time to kill,
Time will stop still for us all one day,
But be left here for others to still dwindle away.

Time is the element, and time always calls,
The ticking of the clock, the time on the wall,
And sometimes it's like a tap slowly dripping away,
Never ending, no respite, every single day,
Time on the wristwatch now broken and smashed,
The hands are motionless, time frozen in the glass.

Walk.

So as I walk through these streets,
I'm always observing all that I see,
The decline of a Country showing,
In the despair and the poverty.

Past vacant buildings that once were pubs,
Vandalised bus shelters, graffitied, then scrubbed,
Passengers huddle against the cold,
Next to advertising boards, faded and old.

Past the derelict houses, with padlocked doors,
Ripped out kitchens with linoleum floors,
Ancient looking buildings were babies scream,
The unemployed sit on steps with faded dreams.

Through these uphill streets with broken concrete,
As the rain beats down, the sewers secrete,
A missing manhole cover, the chances are slim,
Stolen at night and today weighed in.

Tattooed arms are holding evil dogs,
A smashed vodka bottle someones lobbed,
Elastic bands and a single glove,
A wet Valentines card, displaying the love.

As the sky turns black it goes colder still,
Recycled bags and some strange white pills,
In houses with coffee as the t.v blares,
Neighbours are arguing without a care.

The roar of a moped all sounding dead,
An abandoned house with a crumbling shed,
A Police car drives on past, I do not stare,
Yet I can still feel their penetrating glare.

Youths in tracksuits, cardboard gangster dream,
Drinking white cider and acting obscene,
I finally reach home, my hands numb with cold,
The house next door still remains unsold.

Consuming.

Thoughts are like bad drawings, all torn in two,
It's best to share the outrage to the forgotten few,
Like paper that ends up in small bits and pieces,
The consumption of words now suddenly increases.

And with the night-time there arrives empathy,
As we all try to gather together some sympathy,
A consuming vision verging on the madness,
A smile of happiness, a frown built on sadness.

But for the confused, and the enlightened man,
It didn't always turn out just like it began,
We live through experience, search for the cure,
From the day of our birth to our inevitable detour.

I hate the feeling when things start to change,
As life alters, yet stays beautifully arranged,
The inner pouring out of the smallest feelings,
The weak ones amongst us, prone to kneeling.

And in artificial light as all the lines lie,
We look to the moon, we shout up at the sky,
Searching deep in ourselves, emotions run deep,
Looking for answers to consume and to seek.

It seems the words have forever been here,
An untuned concerto, yet still always so clear,
We consume information and put it to the test,
In this life cycle we live, this mad caress.

He keeps Artist hours.

He keeps artist hours,
He feels creative, released,
A canvas and his ideas,
As the paint slowly secretes.

And as people are sleeping,
His head is coming alive,
All the visions are forming,
The smoke rising into his eyes.

Pure white turns to colour,
The shadows and techniques,
The goals he sets himself,
He's never failing to meet.

An empty face has eyes,
A pale hand now with fingertips,
The early hours are rolling by,
A paintbrush, with delicate grip.

And with these early mornings,
With the lost sound of the street,
He continues with his creation,
There's no time for sleep.

A siren from a police car,
A drunk on his way home,
It won't penetrate his consciousness,
He's lost in his thoughts, alone.

And this artwork isn't finished,
Its needing more time to dry,
An adding of more colour,
A touch of emphasis to the sky.

An artist needs the solitary,
A quiet place to contemplate,
A blank canvas turning beautiful,
With his ideas and mixed paint.

For Tim Bennett

Seize the day.

Seize the day,
As you stumble out of bed,
Striking a toe on the settee,
Urine missing the toilet bowl,

As you drink legal stimulant,
That has the nation hooked,
A smell so invigorating,
It could sell a thousand homes.

The door ajar, summer sun cascades,
As the dew hangs on grass blades,
The sky pure blue, unmarked,
Apart from aeroplanes trails,

A criss-cross of oblique designs,
Like the fading scars of Glasgow Gangsters,
The smell of nature, invades the home,
Like a guest you don't recognize.
Seize the day.

Plastic Transparency.

In the shop tonight,
I'm given a transparent carrier bag,
Do you have anything better?,
Do i really need to ask?

And on my way home,
I lift it up into my arms,
So no one can view,
My poverty laden charms.

My sweets for the kids,
Two bags for 50p,
They'll still enjoy them,
Sugar coated confectionery.

And my lager weighing in,
At between three-percent,
It's the best i can do,
I've still to pay the rent.

Chocolate for my Wife,
Two bars for a quid,
Cheap tasting coffee,
With a red plastic lid.

A four pack of toilet rolls,
That looks like cheap paper,
I'm sure they'll be ok,
I'll probably find out later.

Washing up liquid,
That looks like shower gel,
I'll fill up the empty bottles,
I'm sure no one can tell.

And a leaflet inside,
With all the cut price deals,
That butters not a bad price,
It's going for a steal.

Who came up with the idea?,
This window so you can see,
A view into my world,
Through plastic transparency.

The Future

The future is here,
In that small hand you're holding,
In the life lessons they're learning,
The future slowly unfolding.

It's there in the playground,
As they use their imagination,
And the energy in the classroom,
All words, in their formation.

The teaching about the world,
The hands held up in the air,
The future sits cross-legged,
All innocence is laid bare.

These are the people,
That one day will care for us,
Our Doctors, and our Nurses,
Our drivers helping us off the bus.

These aren't just Children,
Playing hop-scotch on concrete,
Like a sponge absorbing ideas,
What we teach, they'll secrete.

The future is our Children,
As we teach them, they will grow,
This is the next generation,
What we reap, they will sow.

ABOUT THE AUTHOR

Steven Michael Pape was born in 1974 in Ilkeston, Derbyshire, England, his first published collection was in 2009; his dark poetry book, 'An Awakening Soul' followed in 2010 with 'Escapism'.

A regular contributor to several publications including newspapers, zines, and FM Anthology a book created in America by the late Poet, Lewis Crystal to highlight the work of poets from around the world. FM is still being edited and published by Rose Terranova Cirigliano today.

Steven has also worked closely with other artists and regularly has his work exhibited with the D.A.N network in England, which highlights artists with disabilities as well as promoting the work of other local poets and artists.

In 2017 Steven teamed up with British photographer Alan Davidson to publish, 'Life in the past frame' a book comprising poems and photos to add the visual aspect to the words, the book was to raise money for the Nightingale Cancer ward in Derby, U.K and a book signing/promotion night was a huge fundraising success.

With this new book,*A weapon called the word*, Steven has written eight books, and continues to write constantly drawing on observations in his life and those around him in society.

He describes the concept of writing poetry as total freedom, a chance to step outside the box and write what he and others are thinking and discussing, that people can hopefully relate to.

Follow on Instagram papepoet74
On Facebook Steven Michael Pape
Email: stevepape16@gmail.com

(photograph by Alan Davidson)

Other works by Steven Michael Pape

Life in the past frame
by Steven Michael Pape and Alan Davidson
Paperback

21st Century Wasteland BIRTH CHAOS DEATH
by Steven Michael Pape and Tim Bennett
Kindle Edition
Paperback

A Closed Mind Is An Open Trap
by Steven Michael Pape
Kindle Edition
Paperback

This Fragile Life
by Steven Michael Pape
Kindle Edition
Paperback